D0520420

by Mary K. Dornhoffer

Content Adviser: Dr. Michael Shannon,
Children's Hospital Boston

Reading Adviser: Dr. Linda D. Labbo,
Department of Reading Education, College of Education,
The University of Georgia

Minneapolis, Minnesota

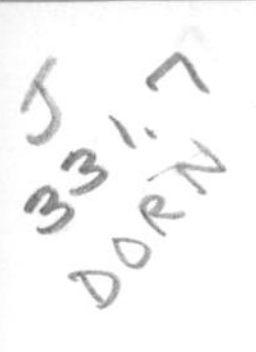

Compass Point Books
3722 West 50th Street, #115
Minneapolis, MN 55410

Visit Compass Point Books on the Internet at *www.compasspointbooks.com* or e-mail your request to *custserv@compasspointbooks.com*

Photographs ©:
International Stock/Scott Campbell, cover; International Stock/Stan Pak, 4; International Stock/Dusty Willison, 5; International Stock/Steve Myers, 6; Leslie O'Shaughnessy, 7; FPG International/Telegraph Colour Library, 8; Visuals Unlimited/SIU, 9; FPG International/Telegraph Colour Library, 10; International Stock/Peter Tenzer, 11; Unicorn Stock Photos/B. W. Hoffman, 12; Photo Network/Mike Moreland, 13; International Stock/Peter Tepper, 14; Leslie O'Shaughnessy, 15; Photo Network/Tom McCarthy, 16; Leslie O'Shaughnessy, 17; Visuals Unlimited/SIU, 18; International Stock/Phyllis Picardi, 19; International Stock/Patrick Ramsey, 20; International Stock/Dusty Willison, 21; Visuals Unlimited/SIU, 22; International Stock/Noble Stock, 23; FPG International/Richard Price, 24; International Stock/ Chuck Mason, 25; FPG International/Bruce Byers, 26; International Stock/Stan Pak, 27.

Editors: E. Russell Primm and Emily J. Dolbear
Photo Researcher: Svetlana Zhurkina
Photo Selector: Linda S. Koutris
Design: Bradfordesign, Inc.

Library of Congress Cataloging-in-Publication Data

Dornhoffer, Mary K.
Doctors / by Mary K. Dornhoffer.
p. cm. — (Community workers)
Includes bibliographical references and index.
Summary: An introduction to the career of doctor, describing the education and training required, different kinds of work they do, and their value to the community.
ISBN 0-7565-0008-7
1. Physicians—Juvenile literature. 2. Medicine—Juvenile literature. [1. Physicians. 2. Occupations.] I. Title. II. Series.
R690 .D674 2000
610.69—dc21 00-008617

Printed in the United States of America.

Table of Contents

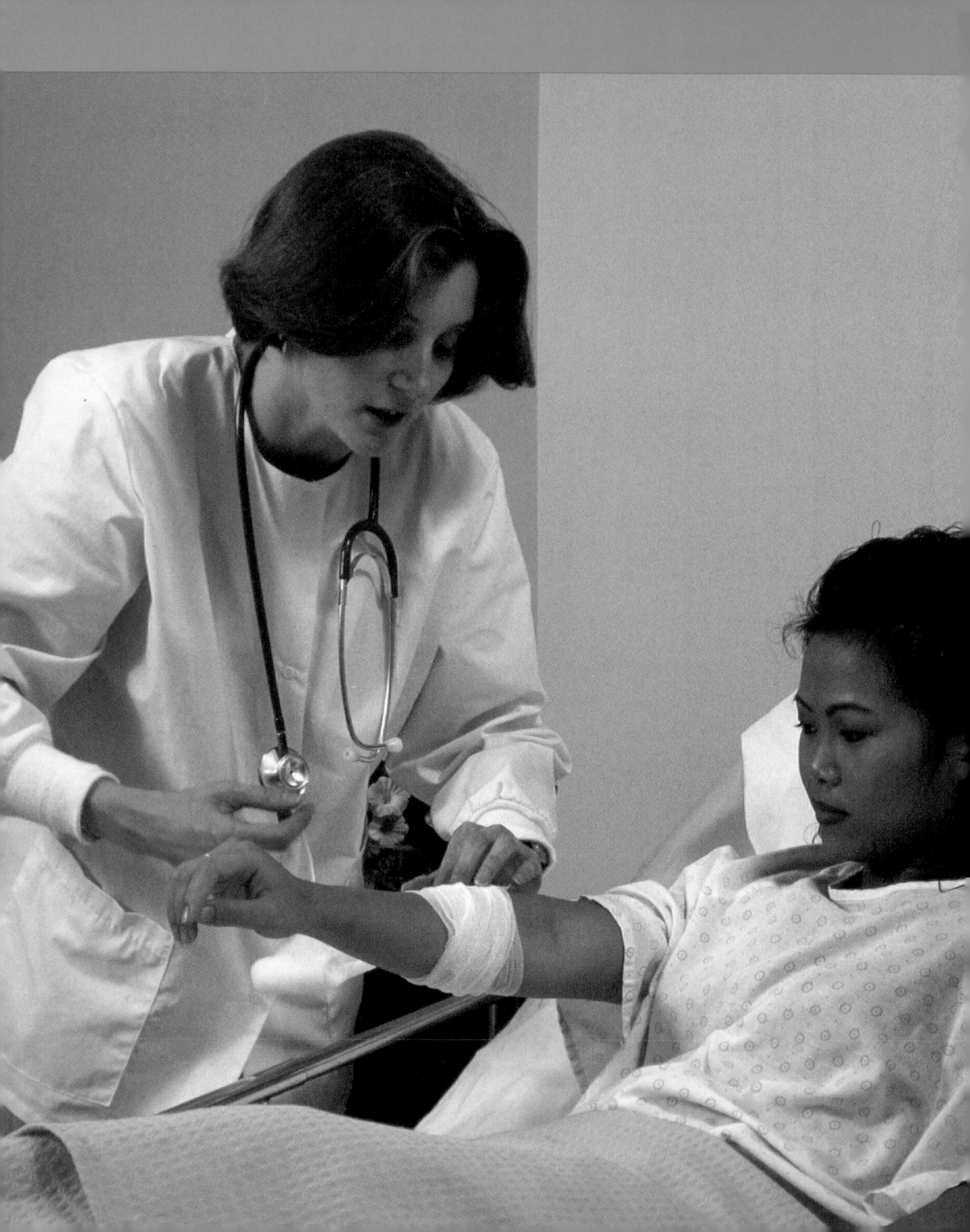

What Do Doctors Do?

Doctors help people who are sick or hurt. They give sick people medicine to help them get well. They fix broken bones and sew up cuts. Doctors also give people **checkups** to make sure they stay healthy.

A doctor with a patient in the hospital

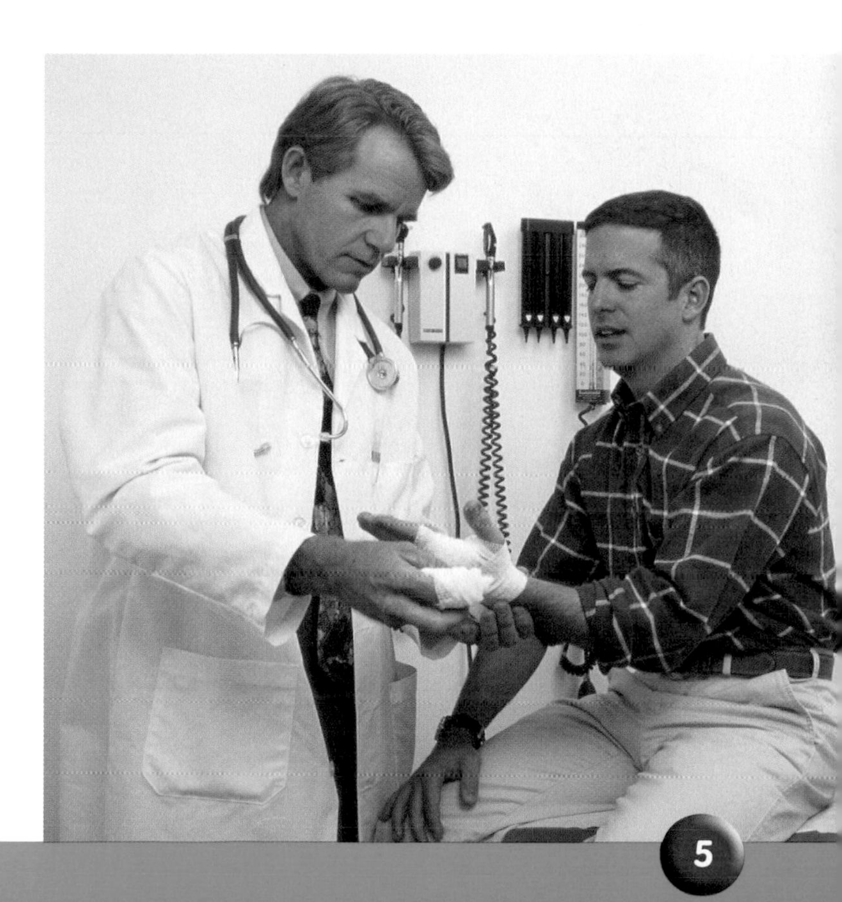

A doctor bandages a patient's hand.

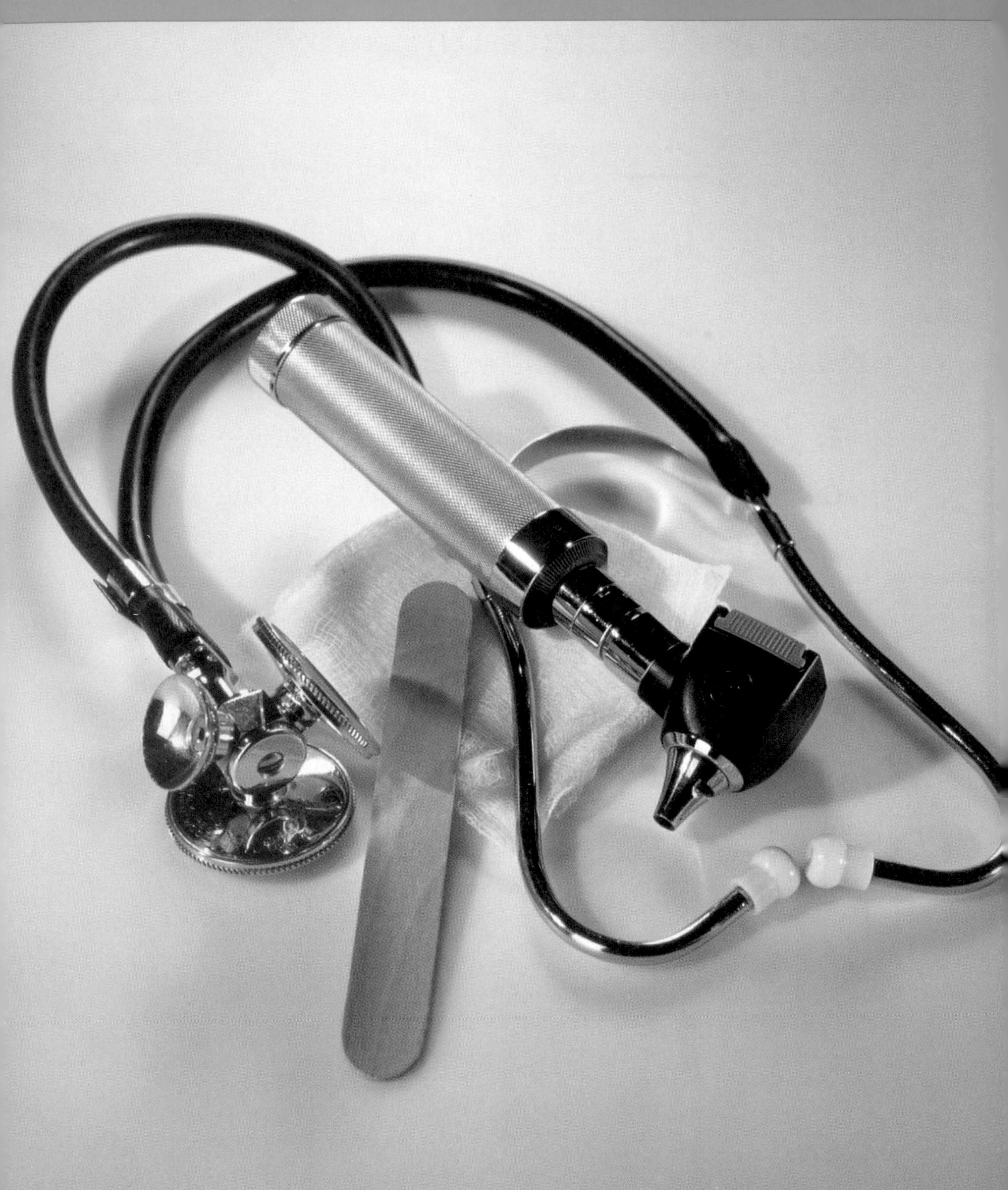

What Tools and Equipment Do They Use?

Doctors carry many tools in their pockets. They use a **stethoscope** to listen to someone's heart and lungs. They have **oto-ophthalmoscopes** to look at a patient's eyes, ears, nose, and throat. Doctors also carry a small rubber hammer to test a patient's **reflexes**.

Medical tools

A doctor checks a boy's ear

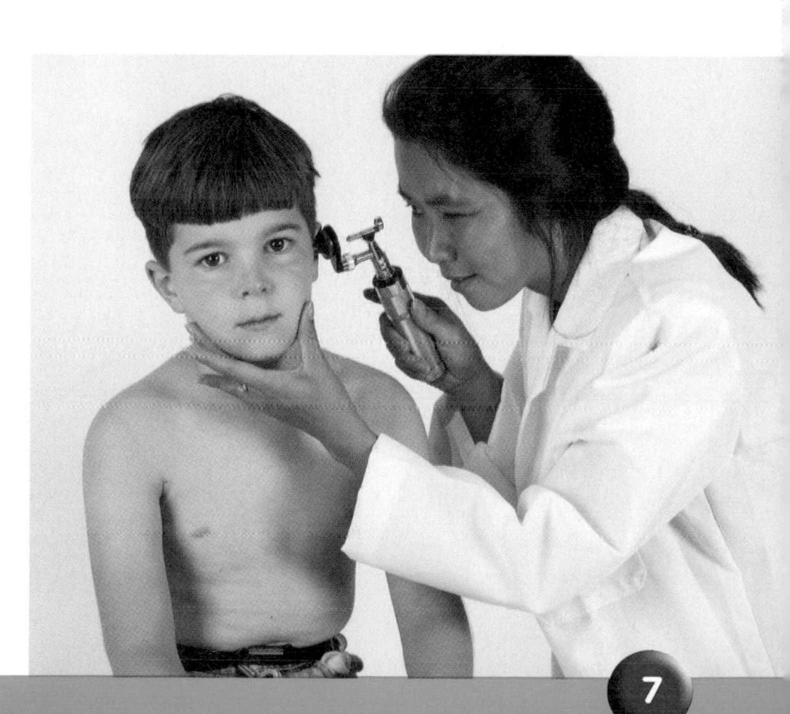

Doctors use tongue depressors to look at someone's throat. They keep the tongue out of the way. Tongue depressors look like popsicle sticks. Doctors also carry pads of paper in their pockets. They use these to write orders for medicine. These orders are called **prescriptions**.

◀ A doctor uses a tongue depressor to look at a girl's throat.

Writing a prescription ▶

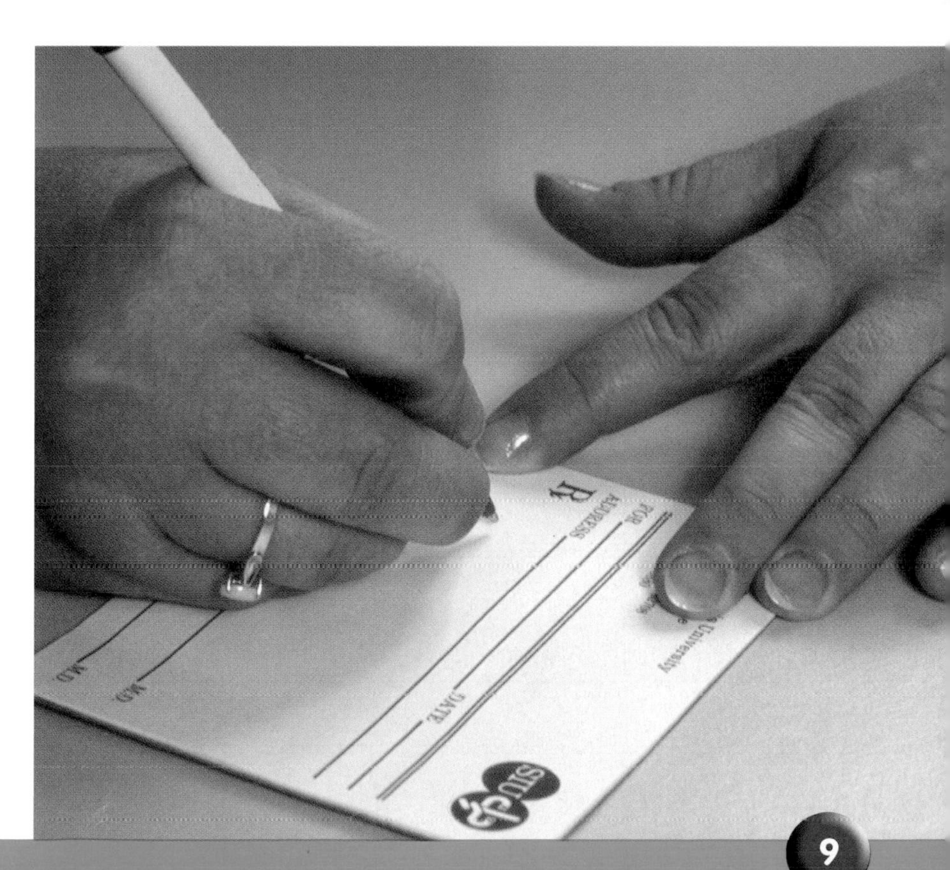

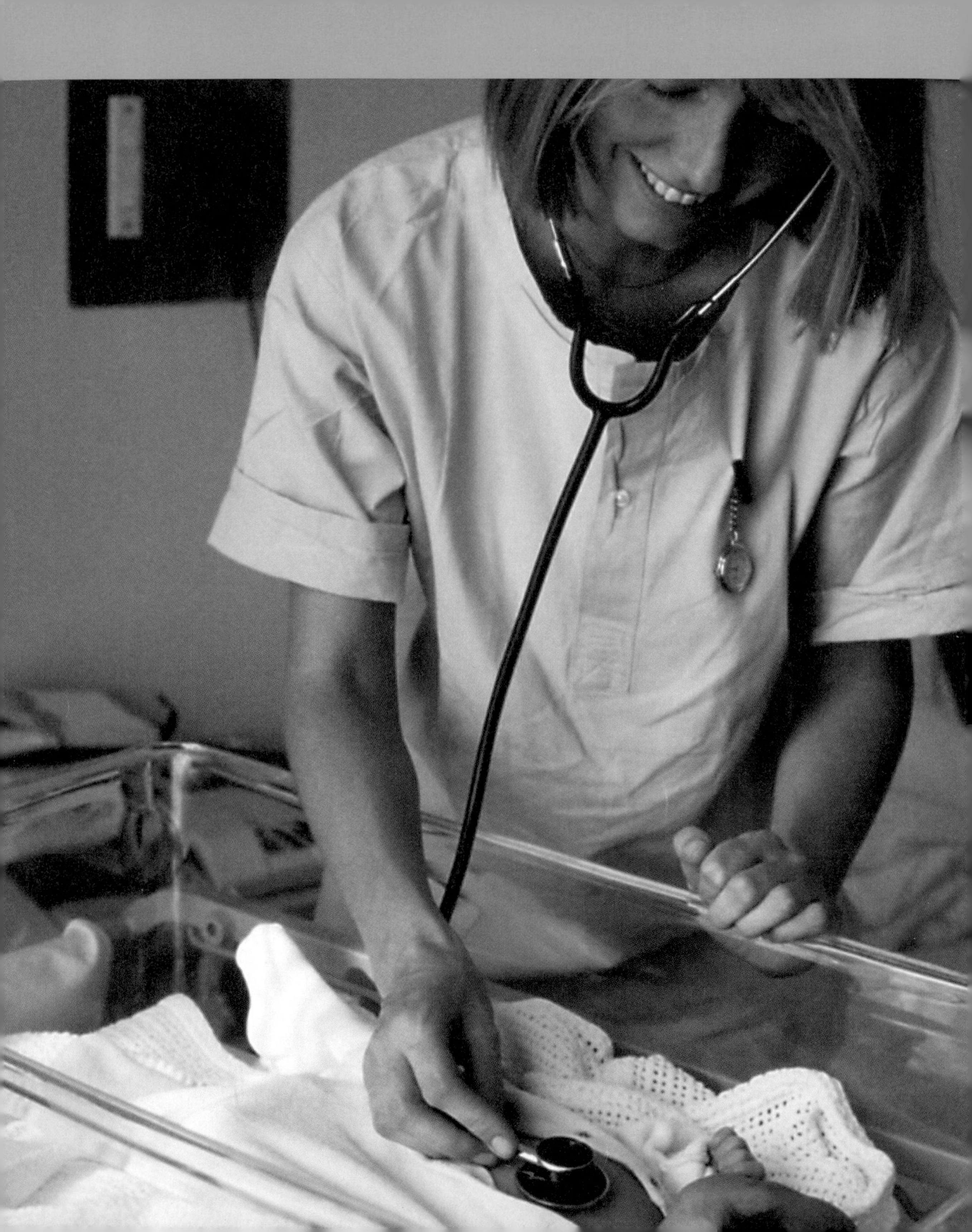

How Do Doctors Help?

Doctors help keep the community healthy. There are more than 150 kinds of doctors. They care for children, pregnant women, and older patients. Doctors are important to everyone.

A doctor examines a newborn baby in a hospital.

A doctor in a laboratory

Where Do They Work?

Some doctors work in laboratories. They study new medicines or search for cures. Some doctors work in the army, navy, or air force. Some doctors work in nursing homes and care for older patients. Others teach new doctors in medical schools.

A doctor uses a skeleton to teach medical students.

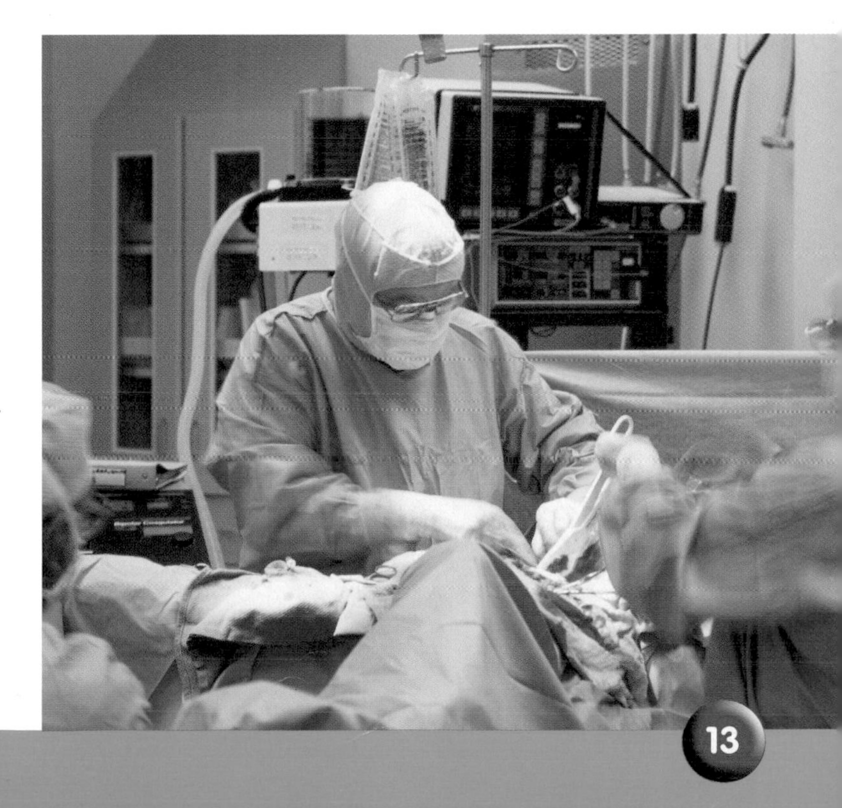

A surgeon during an operation

Who Do They Work With?

Doctors do not work alone. They get help from other doctors, nurses, and physician's assistants. They also work with **paramedics** and many others. All these people work together to help patients.

◀ A paramedic

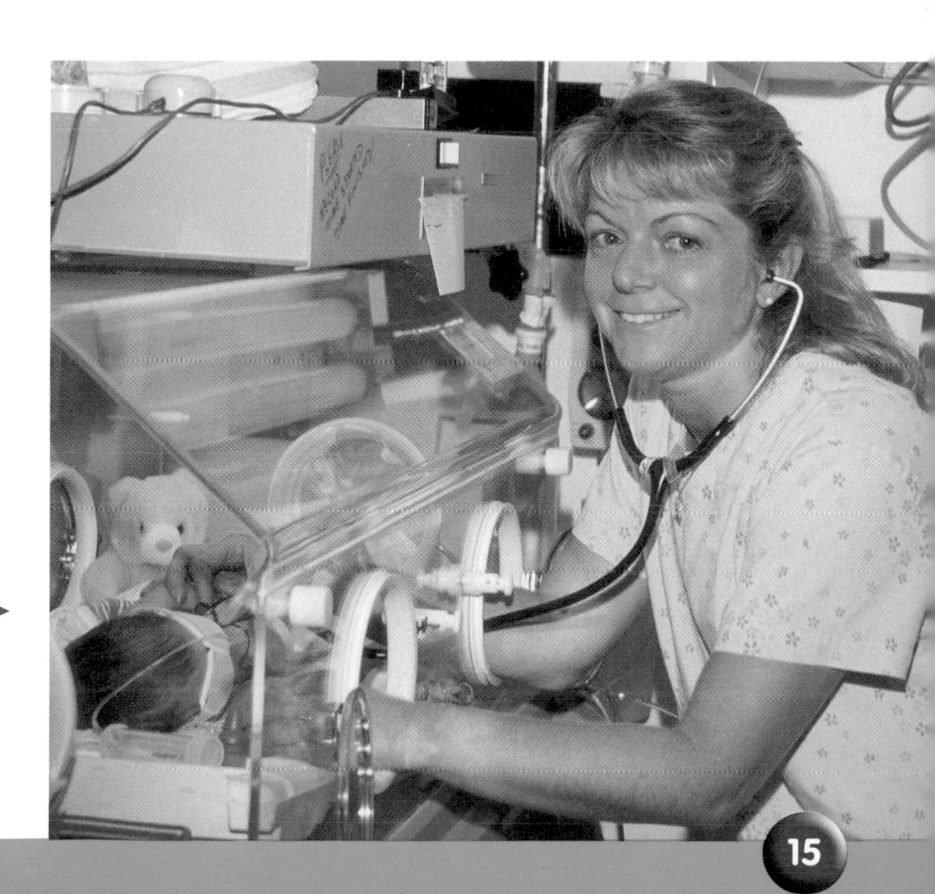

This nurse takes care of babies in a hospital nursery. ▶

What Do They Wear?

In their offices, doctors usually wear a long white coat with lots of pockets. Doctors who do surgery wear scrubs. These look like green or blue pajamas. During surgery, doctors must wear a cap and a mask and put bootees over their shoes. All these things protect the patient from **germs**.

A doctor wears a white lab coat to see patients in his office.

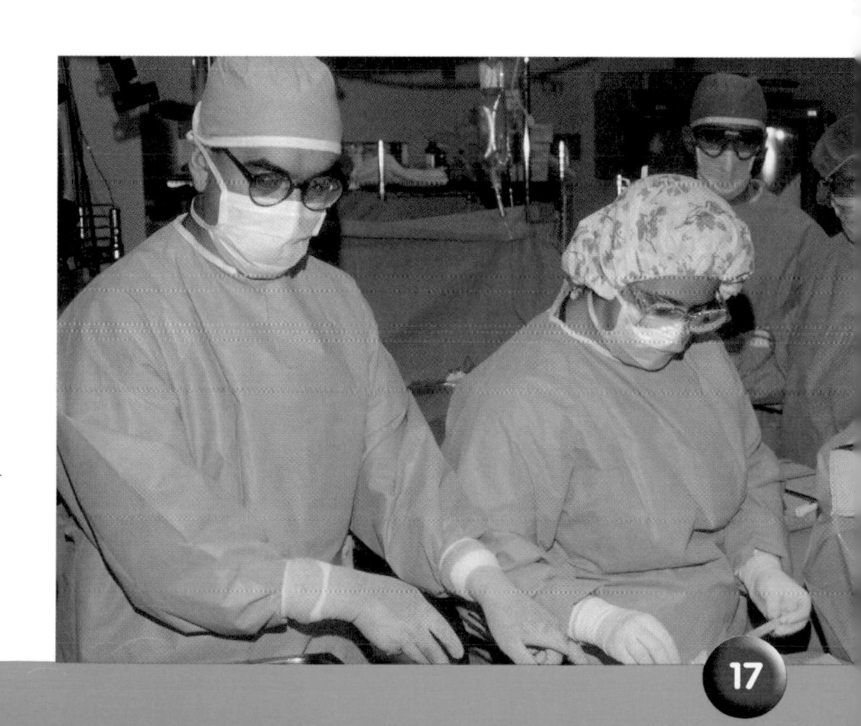

Doctors wear scrubs, surgical masks, and gloves in the operating room.

Infectious Diseases of
INFECTIOUS DISEASES

What Training Does It Take?

First, it takes years of study. Men and women who want to be doctors work hard in high school and college. They study science and math. Then they go to medical school for four years. Medical students learn all about the human body.

◀ A medical student studies at the library.

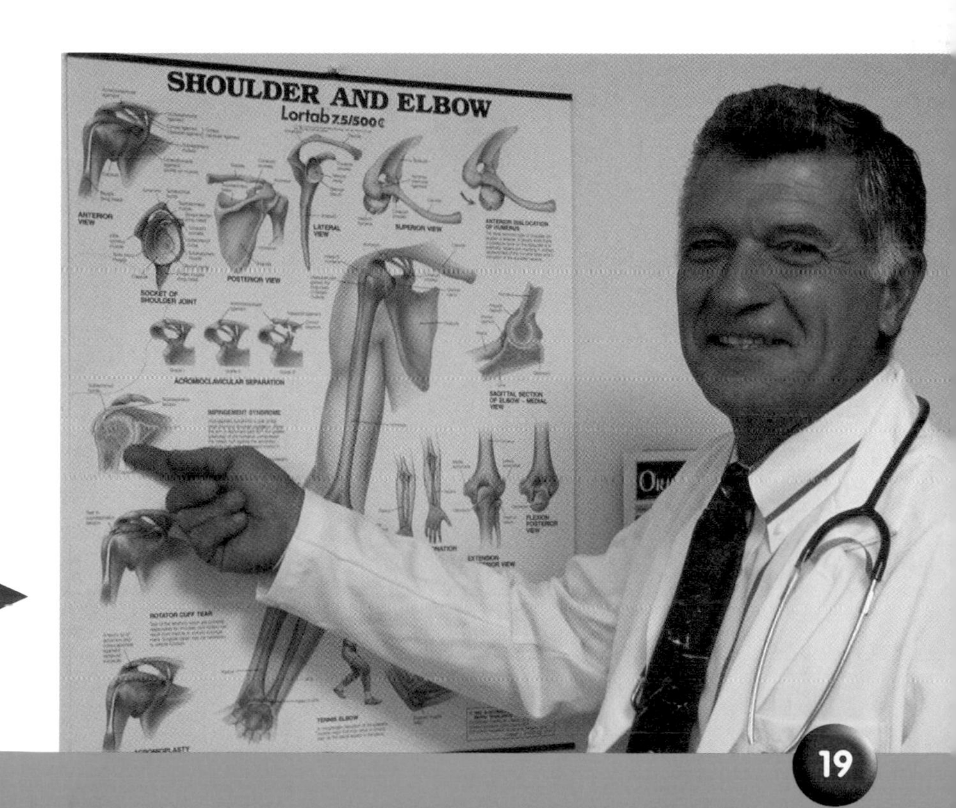

A doctor shows a chart of a shoulder. ▶

What Skills Do They Need?

A good doctor must be a good listener and curious. A good doctor must ask questions and find out why a patient feels sick. A doctor must also know how to make someone feel better.

A doctor listens to her patient.

This doctor uses a teddy bear to make his young patient feel better.

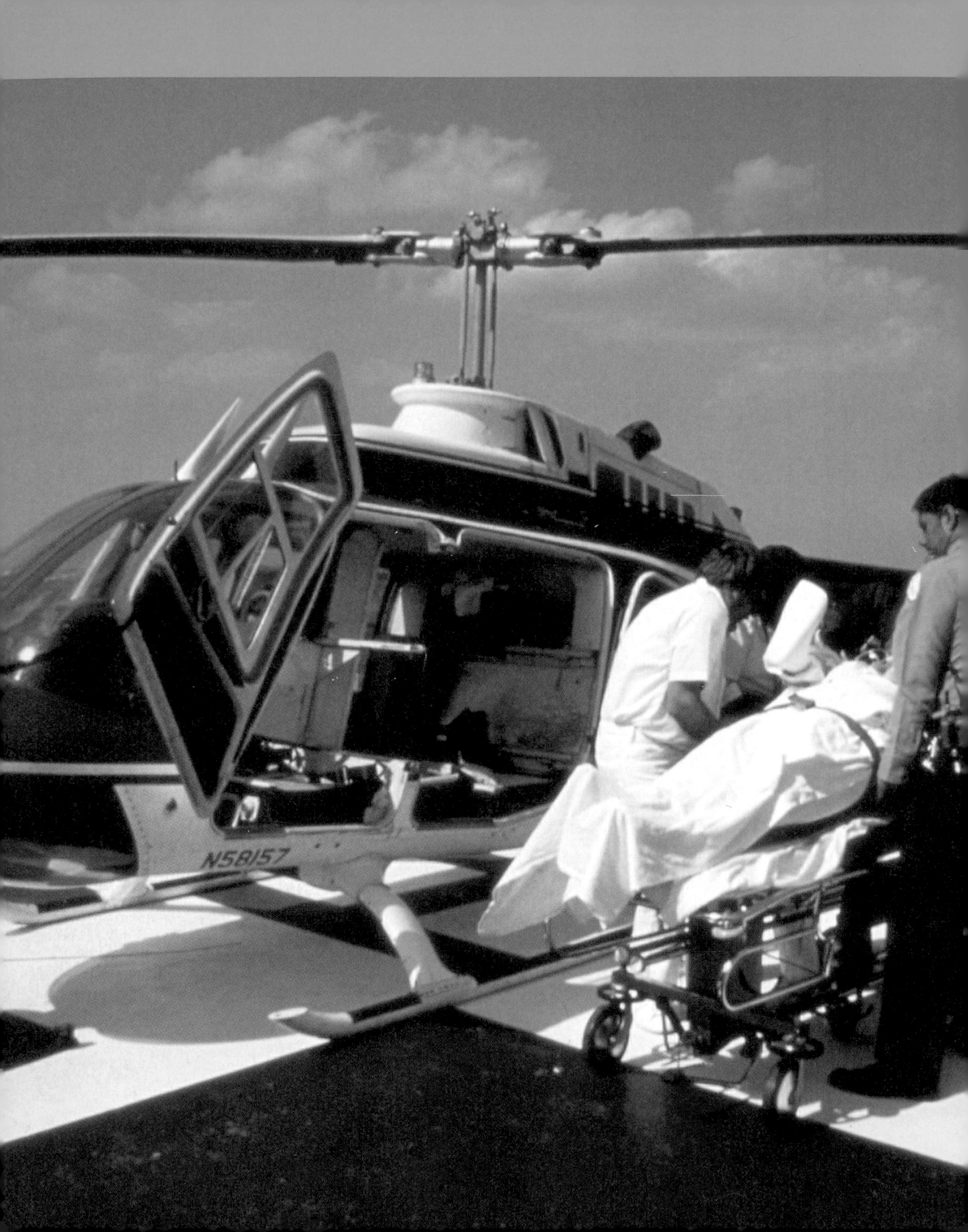
N58157

What Problems Do They Face?

Doctors work long hours into the night. They often have to make important decisions quickly. They face illness and death every day.

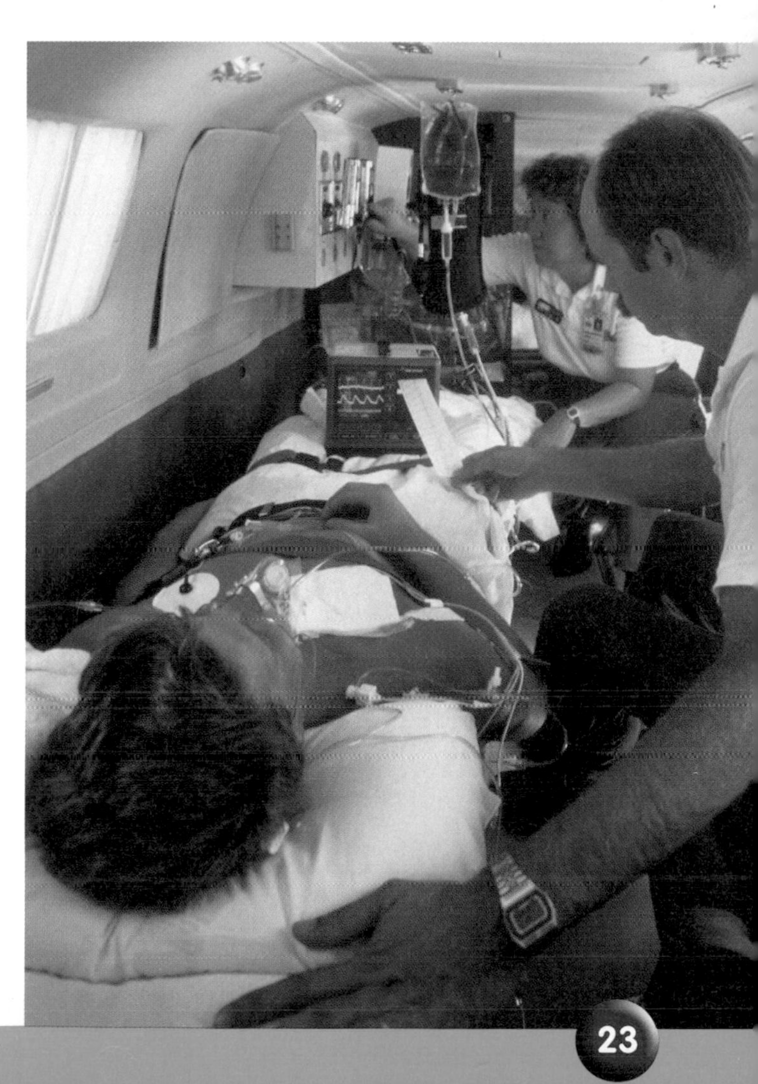

◀ A medical helicopter gets patients to the hospital quickly.

Doctors must treat patients quickly during an emergency. ▶

Would You Like to Be a Doctor?

Do you like helping people? Do you like science? Maybe you would like to be a doctor someday. You can prepare now. In school, study math, science, English, and history. Help others and learn how to solve problems. Be someone who cares about people.

◀ This boy listens to his doctor's heart.

A doctor looks at an X-ray. ▶

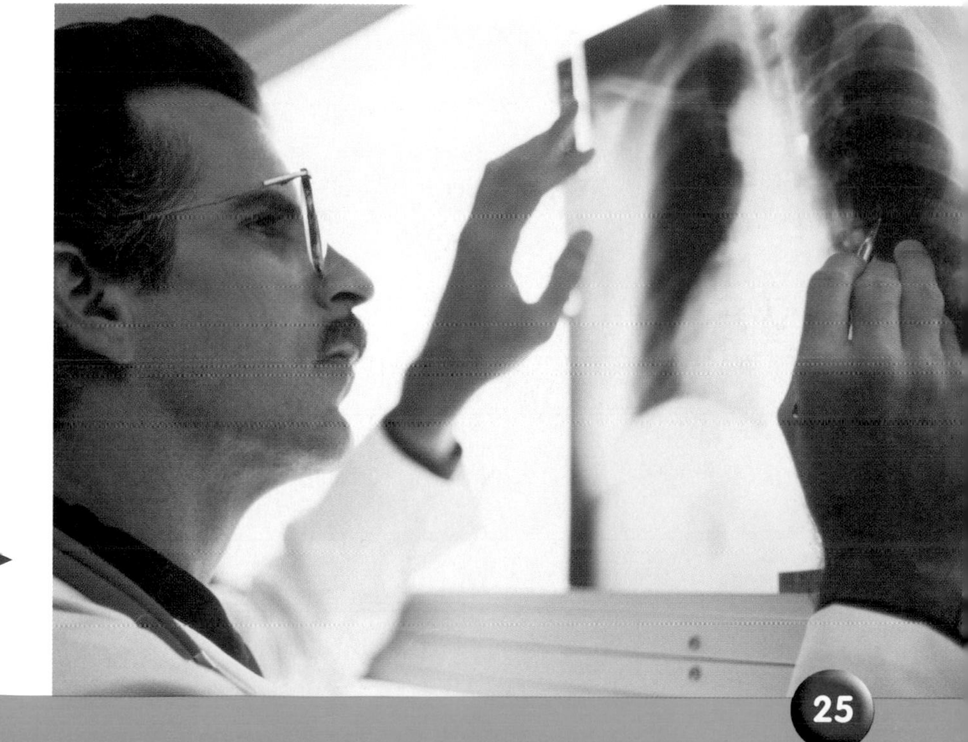

A Doctor's Tools and Clothes

In the Doctor's Office

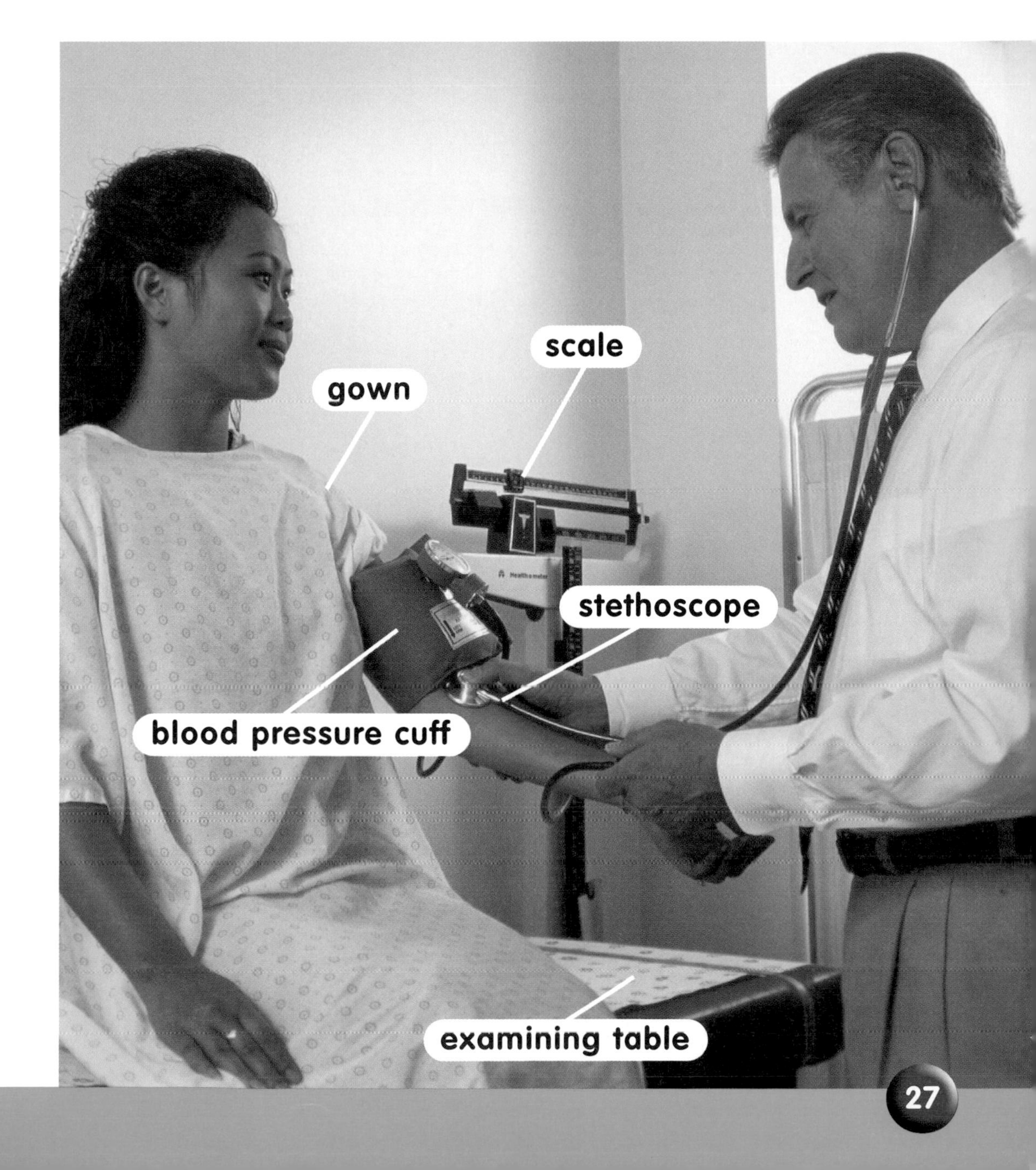

A Doctor's Day

Early morning

- The doctor arrives at the hospital early in the morning. First, she examines her patients and their test results.
- Then, she washes her hands and puts on special clothing for surgery.

Noon

- After surgery, the doctor eats lunch at her desk and logs on to her computer.
- She looks for new medical information. She also fills out patient records.
- Then she visits her patient in the recovery room.

Afternoon

- The doctor goes to the office to see patients for checkups.
- Before examining a patient, she reviews the file.
- She talks to a patient and writes a prescription.

Evening

- The doctor calls the hospital staff and other doctors to check on her patients.

Night

- Late at night, the doctor is called to the hospital emergency room. A doctor's day is never over.

Glossary

checkups—regular visits to the doctor's office

germs—very small living things that cause sickness

oto-ophthalmoscopes—tools that doctors use to look at a patient's eyes, ears, nose, and throat

paramedics—health workers who provide emergency care before or during a trip to a hospital

prescriptions—doctors' orders for medicine

reflexes—natural reactions

stethoscope—a tool doctors use to listen to someone's heart and lungs

Did You Know?

- The first famous doctor was Hippocrates, who lived 2,500 years ago.
- When a person finishes medical school, that person is called "Doctor." A doctor writes the letters "M.D." after his or her name. This stands for Doctor of Medicine.
- More than 560,000 doctors work in the United States.
- It can take more than fifteen years to become a doctor.
- More than 4.2 million people work in health care in the United States.

Want to Know More?

At the Library

Masoff, Joy. *Emergency*. New York: Scholastic, 1999.

Parker, Steve. *Medicine*. New York: Dorling Kindersley, 1995.

Ready, Dee. *Doctors*. Mankato, Minn.: Bridgestone Books, 1997.

On the Web

American Medical Association (AMA)
http://www.ama-assn.org/
The official site of the AMA

KidsHealth
http://kidshealth.org/
A comprehensive site from the experts at the Nemours Foundation

Through the Mail

American Medical Association
515 North State Street
Chicago, IL 60610
For career information about becoming a doctor

On the Road

An easy way to see doctors and other health care workers doing their jobs is to volunteer at a local hospital.

Index

About the Author

Mary K. Dornhoffer has worked as a writer and editor for fifteen years. Before this, she worked as a chemist in a research laboratory. In addition to writing children's books, she is a published poet and has authored technical manuals for laboratory researchers. She enjoys writing children's nonfiction and takes great satisfaction in making challenging subjects interesting to young readers. Mary K. Dornhoffer lives with her husband, John, and her two sons near Little Rock, Arkansas.